P9-DDI-144

EXTREME NATURE

MOUNTAIN EXTREMES

GILLIAN RICHARDSON

Crabtree Publishing Company

www.crabtreebooks.com

Crabtree Publishing Company
www.crabtreebooks.com

Author: Gillian Richardson

Editor: Molly Aloian

Proofreaders: Adrianna Morganelli, Crystal Sikkens, Katherine Berti

Project coordinator: Robert Walker

Production coordinator: Margaret Amy Salter

Prepress technician: Margaret Amy Salter

Project editor: Tom Jackson

Designer: Lynne Lennon

Picture researchers: Sophie Mortimer, Sean Hannaway

Managing editor: Tim Harris

Art director: Jeni Child

Design manager: David Poole

Editorial director: Lindsey Lowe

Children's publisher: Anne O'Daly

Photographs:
Corbis: DLILLC: page 15 (bottom); Galen Rowell: page 26 (center); Hulton-Deutsch Collection: page 27 (top)
Shutterstock: Hiroshi Ichikawa: page 4; Mike Norton: page 5; Galyna Andrushko: pages 6 (left), 11 (bottom), 24-25; Jorg Jahn: page 6 (right); Salamanderman: pages 7 (top), 13 (left), 19 (right); Falk Kienas: page 7 (bottom); Steven Bourelle: pages 8-9; Krzysztof Slusarczyk: page 9; Peter Wey: page 11; Pichugin Dmitry: pages 12-13; Nataliya Hora: page 13 (right); Stephen Finn: pages 14-15; John Kirinic: page 15 (top); John Cronkhite: pages 16-17; Eldad Yitzhak: page 16 (bottom); Graham Prentice: page 17 (bottom); Richard Costin: pages 18-19 (top); Mike Rogal: pages 18-19 (bottom); Fenghui: page 20; Serg Zastavkin: pages 20-21; Danny Warren: page 21 (top); WizData Inc: page 21 (bottom); Enote: pages 22-23; Andrey Plis: page 23; Brian Finestone: page 25 (top); Jason Maehl: page 25 (bottom); Dole: pages 26-27; Dr. Morley Read: page 27 (bottom); Marc van Vuren: page 28; Jeanne Hatch: page 29 (top); Javarman: page 29 (bottom); Rick Parsons: front cover

Illustrations:
Darren Awuah: page 8
BRG: page 10

Every effort has been made to trace the owners of copyrighted material.

Library and Archives Canada Cataloguing in Publication

Richardson, Gillian
Mountain extremes / Gillian Richardson.

(Extreme nature)
Includes index.
ISBN 978-0-7787-4503-7 (bound).--ISBN 978-0-7787-4520-4 (pbk.)

1. Mountain ecology--Juvenile literature. 2. Mountain animals--Juvenile literature. 3. Mountain plants--Juvenile literature. 4. Mountains--Juvenile literature. I. Title. II. Series: Extreme nature (St. Catharines, Ont.)

QH541.5.M65R52 2008 j577.5'3 C2008-907338-X

Library of Congress Cataloging-in-Publication Data

Richardson, Gillian.
Mountain extremes / Gillian Richardson.
p. cm. -- (Extreme nature)
Includes index.
ISBN 978-0-7787-4520-4 (pbk. : alk. paper) -- ISBN 978-0-7787-4503-7 (reinforced library binding : alk. paper)
1. Mountains--Juvenile literature. 2. Mountain ecology--Juvenile literature. I. Title. II. Series.

QH541.5.M65R55 2008
578.75'3--dc22

2008048641

Crabtree Publishing Company
www.crabtreebooks.com 1-800-387-7650

Published in Canada
Crabtree Publishing
616 Welland Ave.
St. Catharines, Ontario
L2M 5V6

Published in the United States
Crabtree Publishing
PMB16A
350 Fifth Ave., Suite 3308
New York, NY 10118

Published in 2009 by CRABTREE PUBLISHING COMPANY.
 In Canada: We acknowledge the financial support of the Government of Canada through the Book Publishing Industry Development Program (BPIDP) for our publishing activities.

CONTENTS

INTRODUCTION

Mountains cover one-fifth of Earth. They even rise up from the ocean floor. The island of Hawaii has five giant mountains. One is Mauna Kea, which rises to 13,796 feet (4,205 m) above the ocean. However, the sides of the mountain drop another 18,192 feet (5,545 m) below the water. That makes Mauna Kea the world's biggest mountain, measuring 6 miles (9.75 km) from top to bottom.

COLD AT THE TOP

The higher you go on a mountain, the colder it gets. As it rises, air spreads out, which makes the temperature cooler. As the air cools, it dries out and spills its moisture as rain—or as snow on higher peaks. Even a mountain in a warm country can have snow on top, such as Japan's Mount Fuji (*right*).

MIGHTIEST PEAKS

The world's highest mountains are in the Himalayas, a massive range of peaks that runs across southern Asia. *Himalaya* means "House of Snow." The range includes the world's highest point. The summit of Mount Everest reaches 29,035 feet (8,850 m). That is the **altitude** at which passenger jets fly.

AMERICAN MOUNTAINS

The longest range in the world are the Andes Mountains. They stretch 4,500 miles (7,420 km) along the west coast of South America. In North America, the Rocky Mountains are almost as long. They link Canada with New Mexico.

EUROPEAN RANGE

Europe's largest range is the Alps, which stretches from southern France to Albania. The word *alpine*, which means "of the mountains," comes from the name of this range.

▼ *The steep-sided Tetons of Wyoming and Idaho are part of the Rocky Mountains.*

SLOW COOKING

At **sea level**, water boils at 212 °F (100 °C). The thinner air at 10,000 feet (3,048 m) makes water boil at lower temperatures—about 194 °F (90 °C). Food cooks slowly at lower temperatures. Therefore, it takes a lot longer to cook food in boiling water if you are camping on a high mountainside.

▼ *Food cooked on high mountains dries out quickly as the water in it boils away. The solution is to keep adding more water—or snow!*

TAKE A BREATH

You normally breathe at a rate of about 20 or 30 breaths every minute. However, on a mountain peak the thin air contains much less **oxygen**. As a result, you have to breathe much faster and more deeply so your body can collect enough oxygen.

CLEAN AND DRY

The higher you go up a mountain, the cleaner the air will become. Most of the dust and **water vapor** that fills the air you breathe is too heavy to be blown high enough to reach the top of a mountain.

▲ *The air at the top of Mount Everest is three times thinner than at sea level. You have to breathe three times as much.*

▲ *The higher you go up a mountain, the windier it gets. The wind is normally twice as strong at 3,000 feet (914 m), as it is at the bottom.*

The cold and dry air damages a climber's lungs. Climbers on Mount Everest call this problem "having the Khumbu Cough."

BURNING RAYS

By the time sunshine reaches sea level, the harmful rays have been filtered out by the **atmosphere**. On a high peak, the light contains twice as much of these harmful rays. The strong sunlight burns the skin and damages the eyes, which can cause blindness.

WHAT SHALL WE WEAR?

In the 20th century, the first people to climb Mount Everest wore woolen clothes and leather boots. Today, climbers wear windproof and waterproof suits stuffed with fibers, mittens, and boots made from woven plastic theads. A lightweight windproof tent and down-filled sleeping bag protect climbers in bad weather.

PLANT LIFE

▶ *Cowberries are similar to cranberries. They grow near mountain peaks.*

A mountaintop is a cold, windy, and often dry place. Temperatures can drop below freezing very quickly. Strong winds blow away the moisture and soil. Mountain plants have to be tough.

HERE TO STAY

Most alpine plants are **perennials**. Perennials grow for years. Some plants loose their leaves and stems for the winter. Alpines have tough stems that remain above the ground all year long. Alpines stop growing in the winter and start again when the weather warms. Many alpine plants save time by reproducing without seeds. They spread out using underground roots.

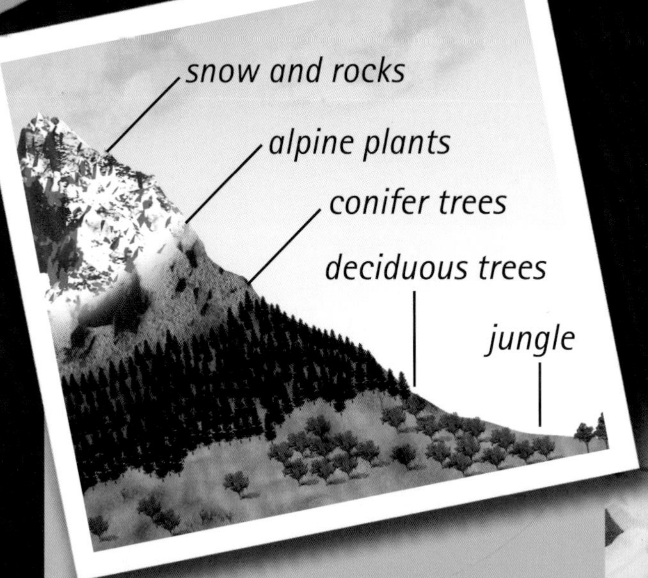

CHANGING ZONES

As you climb a mountain, you will see that the plants change as you get higher—and as the temperature drops. The conditions get tougher as you get higher, so plants suited to the cold survive better. Some mountain bases are covered in jungle. Higher up there is **deciduous** forest, then **conifer** trees. Eventually, it is too cold for any trees to grow. Above this tree line only alpine plants survive. At the very top nothing grows in the permanent snow.

▼ *Leaves of the evergreen Labrador tea plants can be boiled in water to make a spicy drink.*

Vital Statistics

★ Lichens are one of the few plants that live near the tops of mountains.

★ Lichens look like furry mosses covering rocks, and may be brown, white, and even orange!

★ Lichens are actually two life forms living as one: a **fungus** collects water and minerals, while an **alga** turns it into food.

STAYING GREEN

Mountain plants and trees tend to be evergreen—they keep their leaves all winter. Deciduous plants growing further down the mountain drop their leaves so they do not get damaged in the cold. However, alpine plants need to be ready to grow as soon as the weather is warm enough. It would take too long to produce a whole set of new leaves each year.

▲ *A selection of alpine plants from around the world. They all have small, tough leaves.*

HEATING SYSTEM

Alpine plants are able to grow in very cold temperatures. That is because they have ways to trap heat, which helps them grow faster. Dish-shaped flowers track the Sun across the sky to collect as much light and heat as possible. Alpines also have dark colored leaves that absorb warmth.

CLOSE TO THE GROUND

Alpine plants are small and have short stems. They hug the ground in mats or rounded clumps. Being so low allows plants to absorb some heat from the ground. Many take root in sheltered crevices in the rock.

CLINGING ON

The only soil high on a mountain comes from the **erosion** of rock by wind and water. Frozen rocks begin to crack, and flakes of rock and sand form a thin soil. Much of it blows away. Only small plant **species** with shallow roots are able to grow.

SAVING WATER

The leaves of alpine plants have waxy coatings, which stops them from drying out in the wind. Their leaves are also often hairy. The fine hairs trap heat and keep out the wind. The hairs also reflect or **absorb** the harmful rays in the bright sunlight that would normally scorch the plant.

▶ *In the summer, the weather gets warm enough for the empty mountainside to burst into color as the plants flower.*

In the Extreme

In the Andes, the Incas farmed the only crops that grew at high altitude—potatoes. They grew in fields cut into the mountains, such as at Machu Picchu in Peru. Potato plants survive the cold, strong winds, and heavy snow because they grow close to the ground. The soil is dry, so the plants collect extra water from mist using short hairs on their leaves.

THE HILLS ARE ALIVE

An alpine meadow is a grassland that grows at high altitude. For most of the year, it is covered in snow. In spring, warm winds blow up the mountain and melt the snow. As soon as the ground is uncovered, a carpet of brightly colored flowers burst open to attract insects for **pollination**.

MAKING FOOD

Plants make food by **photosynthesis**. They use sunlight to make sugar from the **carbon dioxide** in the air. Alpines must make enough food in the summer to last all year. They store it in their stems or rounded roots for the long winter.

▼ *Valleys are often in shadow beneath the ridges. That means plants in the valleys may grow more slowly, but they are also sheltered from the worst of the weather.*

Vital Statistics

★ Edelweiss is a star-shaped flower that lives in the Alps.

★ The name *edelweiss* means "noble white"—the petals are white, but the center of the flower is yellow.

★ The leaves have fines hairs that make the plant look woolly.

Vital Statistics

★ Rhododendron is a large bush that grows on high rocky slopes in the Himalayan Mountains.

★ Its name means "red tree" after the large red flowers that color the steep hillsides (below).

★ The plant is the national flower of Nepal.

MAKE A POINT

Conifer trees, such as fir, cedar, spruce, and pine, are adapted to life in cold weather. They have a strong central trunk, and their branches stick out in all directions to form a pointed cone shape. The cone stands firm in the wind, and snow slides down its sides so it does not weigh down the tree.
A conifer's leaves are thin needles. The needles stay on the tree all year so it is ready to start growing again in spring. The needle-shaped leaves will not freeze in winter.

ANIMAL LIFE

Animals need food, water, and shelter—there is not much of these on mountains. Only **warm-blooded** animals and a few insects live there all the time. Other animals are just visitors. They **migrate** up and down as the seasons change.

▼ *Highland cattle from Scotland have long, shaggy coats that keep them warm out in the open in winter.*

KEEPING OUT THE COLD

Mountain animals must be **insulated** from freezing temperatures and winds. Most animals have thick fur or fat under the skin. They also have short legs, tails, and small ears to reduce heat loss.

STEADY FEET

Leaping confidently across steep rocky slopes and up cliffs would be impossible for the bighorn sheep without its incredible hooves. Hard outer edges cut into ice, while spongy pads underneath help the sheep grip as it climbs up the steepest slopes far away from **predators.**

UP AND DOWN

Once the snow has melted, goats and deer climb up to feed in alpine meadows. As winter approaches, their food becomes hard to find. The animals head down to shelter in warmer valleys.

Vital Statistics

- The largest cat in the Himalayas is the snow leopard.
- The cat's gray coat has dark rings, which help it blend in with rocks as it stalks wild sheep.
- The long tail helps the big cat balance as it charges over rocks toward its **prey**.

SAVING HEAT

Being darkly colored is best for mountain animals because it helps the body absorb heat in sunlight. Pale colors reflect light and heat. Hairless skin, such as on the tip of the nose, is always dark. This helps prevent **frostbite**.

STAYING OUT OF SIGHT

Darkly colored animals might be warmer, but they are also very easy to see when surrounded by white snow. That puts them at risk of attack from predators, such as cougars, leopards, and eagles. Some animals change color to match the rocks and snow of the mountainside.

MOUNTAIN PARROT

You may think of parrots as birds of the tropical rain forests. However, the kea is the world's only alpine parrot. It lives in the mountains of southern New Zealand. The bird feeds above the tree line on just about anything, such as insects, berries, and nectar, and they even pick at dead animal bodies.

CHANGING COLORS

The ptarmigan lives in the Rocky Mountains. Its feathers turn white for **camouflage** while the snow is on the ground. It **molts** these feathers once the snow melts, changing them to a mixture of gray, brown, and black which helps it hide on the rocky ground.

INSECT SURVIVORS

Most insects cannot move when it is even slightly cold. However, snow flies are still active at 23 °F (-5 °C). The insects have **antifreeze** in their blood, which stops ice from forming inside the body.

◀ *A ptarmigan has warm "boots" made from feathers around its feet.*

In the Extreme

The alpine weta of New Zealand is a giant cricket. It cannot fly—it is too windy in the mountains. It **hibernates** under rocks in winter. Some alpine wetas even freeze solid as they wait out the bad weather. The insects survive because only the water around the body **cells** freezes. The water inside the cells stays liquid.

Vital Statistics

★ The Andean condor has the largest wings of any bird.

★ The condor glides up to 18,000 feet (5,486 m) on warm air currents over the mountains of South America.

★ The sharp-eyed bird looks for the bodies of dead animals, such as sheep or llamas.

▶ *A bar-headed goose; this type of goose flies over the Himalayas twice a year.*

RED BLOOD

Animals living on the world's highest mountains breathe air that contains half of the oxygen we get at sea level. Mountain creatures have a lot more **red blood cells**. This allows them to collect more oxygen in each breath.

HIGH FLYERS

The bar-headed goose crosses the Himalayas from India to its nesting grounds in Tibet each spring. As with all birds, each breath runs through the lungs to air sacs.

In the Extreme

The yak is a wild relative of cattle. It is one of the highest-living mammals and is found at 16,400 feet (5,000 m). The yak's shaggy coat allows it to survive freezing temperatures, and it has huge lungs so it can breathe in large amounts of the thin air. The yak's hooves are split into two large toes that grip the slippery ground. Horns help it dig under the snow for grass and roots.

The birds' air sacs allow air to flow into the lungs faster so the birds can get oxygen more quickly. Bar-headed geese also have special hemoglobin. This blood chemical is able to pick up oxygen even from thin mountain air.

SLEEP THROUGH IT

A large squirrel called a marmot has found a good way to survive in alpine meadows. It hibernates in the warmth and safety of a burrow. It goes to sleep for eight months—from September to May. Talk about sleeping in! The animal is only awake in summer—just as the meadow plants are at the tastiest.

FOOD STORE

Pikas make sure they can eat in winter by hoarding food during the summer. They gather grasses from alpine meadows and dry them under rocks. In winter, the pikas tunnel through the snow to reach their stores of hay.

▼ *A pika is a small relative of a rabbit. It has very thick fur, which makes its body look very round.*

Vital Statistics

★ Giant pandas make their home in the remote forests growing on the mountains of central China.

★ Pandas eat bamboo, a type of thick grass that grows on the slopes.

★ Pandas spend summer high up, but move down to valleys in winter.

MOUNTAIN CAMELS

High mountains are very dry—all the liquid water is solid ice—so it helps to be able to go without water for a long time. Llamas live in the Andes. They have three stomach chambers which can absorb the water they need from the leaves they eat. A thick coat keeps them warm. Long necks allow llamas to keep a sharp eye out for cougars and other predators.

In the Extreme

Snow monkeys have learned to live in the cold northern areas of Japan's Nagano Mountains by warming themselves in natural hot springs around the Shiga Kogen volcano. Besides adapting to the cold, these monkeys live on a varied **diet**. In winter, twigs and bark are their main foods.

MOUNTAIN PEOPLE

Living on a high mountain is difficult for most people. People who were born at high altitudes are better suited for it. However, even they cannot survive for long on the world's highest peaks, which are named the Death Zone.

▼ *The Potala Palace in Lhasa, Tibet, was first built 1,300 years ago. It was later burned down by a lightning strike and rebuilt in 1645.*

GAS WORKS

Your body needs a supply of oxygen. Air is a mixture of gases. About one-fifth of it is oxygen. As you climb a mountain, the weight of Earth's atmosphere, measured as **air pressure**, goes down. At low pressure, the gases spread out—the air gets thinner. You must breathe in a lot more air to get enough oxygen for your muscles and brain to work properly.

HIGH LIVING

Mountain people have larger lungs to take in more air in each breath. They also have more red blood cells in the body to make it easier to collect more oxygen from the thin air.

BODY CHANGES

If a person raised at sea level comes to live in the mountains, his or her body will eventually change to deal with the thinner air. The body makes more blood cells so his or her blood becomes darker. Athletes train in the mountains before a big race. The extra blood cells they make there will help them compete faster and for longer back down at sea level.

COUNTDOWN

How long could you survive at the top of Mount Everest? In the thin air, you will pass out in a few minutes. Your brain swells up and your lungs begin to dry out. You are too heavy for rescuers to carry down, and the cold will kill you in a couple of hours.

GETTING SICK

Above 8,200 feet (2,500 m), people are at risk for altitude sickness, also called acute mountain sickness. It starts because your body cannot get enough oxygen. You become dizzy, get headaches, and feel like vomiting. You have to breathe hard even when lying down—that makes it hard to sleep. The only cure is to go back down the mountain.

WATER ON THE BRAIN

The problems get worse as you get higher. Above 26,250 feet (8,000 m) is known as the Death Zone. Up there people get HACE, which stands for High-Altitude Cerebral Edema. That is the scientific way of saying that the liquid part of the blood is leaking into the brain. The liquid squeezes the brain, and climbers cannot walk or talk. A sufferer is also too confused to realize what is happening. He or she must be helped down the mountain, or will die within hours.

▼ *Mountain climbing is a lot of fun, but it is also very dangerous. Only experts can make it to the top of the tallest peaks safely.*

TAKING TIME

The best way of avoiding these problems is to move up the mountain slowly, so your body can get used to the conditions. This can take several days. Climbers on Everest have to stop for a good rest after going up every 1,000 feet (304 m).

In the Extreme

Helicopters cannot fly very well above 18,000 feet (5,486 m) because the air is too thin to lift the aircraft up. However, a helicopter can hover above a peak on a cushion of thick air that it creates with its rotor blades. The farther it moves away from the peak, the weaker that cushion becomes, so the pilot must fly down fast, or risk falling out of the sky!

LEAKING LUNGS

If climbers go up too fast, their blood leaks into the lungs. That makes it difficult for them to breathe—they may even drown! Climbers spend a few days at a base camp so their bodies get used to the altitude.

ALPINE FARMERS

Certain breeds of cattle or sheep can graze in alpine meadows in summer. However, it is much more difficult to grow crops on high slopes. In the Andes and Himalayas, people have solved the problem by building terraced fields, or wide flat steps built on the mountainside.

▼ *Vietnam is a mountainous country. Over the centuries, people have turned the steep slopes into terraces for growing rice.*

KILLER PEAK

The world's second-highest mountain is K2 (right) in the Karakoram Range of Pakistan and China. At 28,251 feet (8,611 m) it is not quite as high as Everest. However, it is much more dangerous to climb because it is so steep and the weather can get very cold without warning. Only 280 people have made it to the top so far. However, 66 of them died on the way back down!

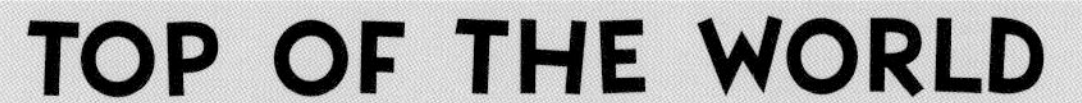

TOP OF THE WORLD

New Zealand climber Sir Edmond Hillary (*pictured, left*) is the first person known to reach the summit of Mount Everest, along with his guide, a Tibetan named Tenzing Norgay (*right*). Hillary and Norgay made the climb in 1953. A British climber named George Mallory may have reached the top in 1924, but died on the mountain. In 1999, Mallory's frozen body was found close to the summit. No one knows whether he died on the way up or down.

FAST FACTS

★ Toothache is a big problem for climbers who have air trapped in their fillings. The air inside is at a higher pressure than the thin mountain air. The air tries to escape causing a lot of pain. The filling might pop right out!

★ A lahar (*left*) is a mudslide caused by a volcano. In 1985, the town of Amero in Colombia, South America, was buried by a lahar. The mud killed 23,000 people in seconds.

EXTREME FACTS

TESTING THE AIR
Lichens are called bioindicators. That means they are very sensitive to **pollution** in the air. Even tiny amounts will kill them. If lichens are growing somewhere, the air must be clean.

HIDDEN PEAK
If you placed Mount Everest, the highest peak on Earth, into the deepest part of the ocean—the Challenger Deep in the Pacific's Mariana Trench—its summit would still be covered by 6,500 feet (1,981 m) of sea water.

HOT COLORS
People living high in the Andes have adapted to mountain life by having more hemoglobin in their blood. However, the Tibetan people (*right*) from the Himalayas have larger blood vessels instead.

RECORD BREAKER
The large-eared pika, a relative of the rabbit, is the highest-living mammal. It has been found living at 20,111 feet (6,130 m) in the mountains of China.

HOT COLORS
A red or blue **pigment** in alpine plants, called anthocyanin, can convert light into heat.

STILL GROWING
Mount Everest grows 0.16 inches (4 mm) every year. Scientists believe the forces that created the Himalayas are still pushing upward from deep under the ground, forcing the land even higher.

TELESCOPE MOUNTAIN

The summit of Mauna Kea in Hawaii is covered with giant telescopes (*left*). There are 12 in all, run by scientists from around the world. The air above the mountain is very clear and the weather is just right for looking at the stars.

TOP CAPITAL

La Paz, Bolivia, is the world's highest capital city. The city (*right*) is 11,811 feet (3,600 m) up in the Andes. The city's airport is even higher at 13,325 feet (4,061 m) in the suburb of El Alto. It is the highest international airport in the world.

HIDDEN RANGE

The longest mountain range is hidden under an ocean. The Mid-Ocean Ridge runs for 52,000 miles (84,000 km) from the North Atlantic through the Indian Ocean and into the Pacific. The mountain range breaks the surface at Iceland and the Azores.

GLOSSARY

absorb To take in

air pressure The measure of how hard the air is pressing down on you

alga A tiny life form similar to a plant

altitude A measure of how high you are

antifreeze A chemical that stops water from turning into ice

atmosphere The gases around Earth

camouflage Colors that help an animal stay hidden in the wild

carbon dioxide A gas produced as waste by the body

cells The tiny units that make up organisms

conifers Trees such as pines and firs

deciduous Trees that drop their leaves at certain times of year

diet What an animal eats

erosion When rock is worn away

frostbite An injury to skin caused by cold temperatures

fungus A type of living thing that includes mushrooms and molds

hibernates Sleeps through the winter

insulated Covered to keep the cold out

migrate To travel from one place to another each year

molts To lose hair or feathers

oxygen A gas in the air used by living bodies to burn food

perennials Plants that live for many years

photosynthesis The way plants make sugar from carbon dioxide and water

pigment A colored chemical

pollination The way plants make seeds when pollen in transferred between flowers. Insects usually carry pollen

pollution Something that is harmful to the environment

predator An animal that hunts other animals

prey An animal that is hunted by another animal

red blood cells The cells in blood that carry oxygen

sea level The point from which the height of mountains is measured

species A group of animals that are very closely related to each other

warm-blooded An animal that keeps its body at a fixed temperature

water vapor Steam; water as a gas

FURTHER RESOURCES

BOOKS

101 Facts About Mountains by Julia Barnes. Milwaukee, WI: Gareth Stevens Publishing, 2004.

America's Mountains by Frank Staub. New York, NY: Mondo Publishing, 2003.

Life at a High Altitude by Judy Levin: New York, NY: Rosen Central, 2004.

Living in the Mountains by Neil Morris. North Mankato, MN: Smart Apple Media, 2004.

Mountain Explorer by Greg Pyers. Chicago, IL: Raintree, 2005.

Mountains by Margaret Hynes. New York, NY: Kingfisher, 2007.

WEBSITES

National Geographic's Mountain page

science.nationalgeographic.com/science/earth/surface-of-the-earth/mountains-article.html

Panoramic View from Mount Everest (Try fullscreen)

www.panoramas.dk/Fullscreen2/Full22.html

The Seven Summits (slide show of highest peaks on each continent)

www.pbs.org/wgbh/nova/kilimanjaro/seven.html

INDEX

Printed in the U.S.A. – BG